HELP
YOUR
CHILD
MAKE
FRIENDS

HELP YOUR CHILD MAKE FRIENDS

An Hachette UK Company
www.hachette.co.uk

Vie Books, an imprint of Summersdale Publishers Ltd
Part of Octopus Publishing Group Limited
Carmelite House
50 Victoria Embankment
LONDON
EC4Y 0DZ
UK

www.summersdale.com

Printed and bound in Poland

ISBN: 978-1-78783-665-5

Substantial discounts on bulk quantities of Summersdale books are available to corporations, professional associations and other organizations. For details contact general enquiries: telephone: +44 (0) 1243 771107 or email: enquiries@summersdale.com.

HELP YOUR CHILD MAKE FRIENDS

101 Ways to Nurture Healthy and Happy Friendships

POPPY O'NEILL

Disclaimer

CONTENTS

How to Use This Book

Recent research conducted by the British Psychological Society suggests that childhood friendships have a marked effect on lifelong mental and emotional health. They're also one of the main places we learn to build connections with others – skills that inform how we later form adult relationships.

If you're a parent or carer concerned about the quantity or quality of your child's friendships, you're not alone. The importance of our young people's social development is gaining more and more recognition among psychologists, teachers and in the media.

Taking a broad view of childhood friendships from ages 5–16, this book gathers advice and techniques from professionals and boils them down into practical, easy-to-apply tips.

You know your child best, so pick and choose the advice that resonates with you.

INTRODUCTION

For children, social interactions and expectations can be confusing! Things like rejection, big life changes, sensitivity and shyness can impact children's ability to make or keep friends. Without guidance, children might feel helpless and baffled by the ups and downs of friendships.

While every child (and every friendship) is different, if your child is struggling you may notice some of these common signs:

- **They tell you they don't have any friends.**
- **Reluctance to go to school.**
- **Tumultuous or short-lived friendships.**
- **Social anxiety.**
- **Withdrawing from or turning down social invitations.**

If these sound familiar, don't panic. There is a lot you can do to help your child build a healthy, fulfilling social life. Read on for a wealth of ideas and advice.

CHAPTER 1

Grow Your Child's Confidence and Self-Esteem

The foundations of good friendships come from a positive relationship with ourselves. When self-esteem is high, a child is resilient, confident and makes good choices about whom they spend their time with. When a child believes they are unlikeable, it forms a barrier to making friends, even if potential friends are right in front of them. In this chapter we'll look at activities, conversations and ideas you can try with your child to help grow their self-esteem and be a good friend to themselves first.

You don't have to be perfect to deserve good friends

If your child suffers with low self-esteem, it may be difficult for them to understand why someone might want to be friends with them. They might be hard on themselves if they make a mistake, or act awkward or shy around others.

Let them know that even when they make a mistake, even when they say the wrong thing or mess up, even on their worst days they still deserve good, supportive friends, and that they are still loveable and likeable.

Be a good friend to yourself first

In order to overcome difficulties making friends, it's useful to explain the idea of being your own best friend to your child. This idea can be applied in the way we think and speak about ourselves as well as the choices we make.

A good time to talk about this is when they've made a mistake, like tripping over in public. It's possible that your child could be mentally beating themselves up about it – notice the words they might use about themselves in these moments and counter them with a kinder perspective.

Each time your child hears a friendlier, more generous view of themselves, they will learn more about how to be a friend as well as what kind of treatment to expect from a friend.

How does your child think about themselves?

Thinking negatively about ourselves often comes hand in hand with low self-esteem. Notice the words your child uses and the things they assume to be true about themselves.

Gently challenge your child when they talk themselves down. Rather than telling them they're wrong, it is often more useful to suggest an alternative view. This way, your child's mind becomes open to the possibility of choosing a new perspective, rather than accepting that one perspective is absolutely true.

Taking care of ourselves

Aside from being essential to good health, treating our bodies with respect has a knock-on effect. When we look after our bodies well, we learn to treat our emotions and the people in our lives with the same care.

The level of independence you expect from your child will depend on their age. However, erring on the side of independence is always a positive choice. Taking time to teach your child *why* we clean our teeth or change our underwear, as well as how to do it, will encourage independence.

Building strong values

When we have integrity, our actions match up with our beliefs. When we know what's important to us, we feel comfortable being ourselves, inside and out. Having integrity means we are strong-minded and trustworthy – two attributes of a good friend.

Try this activity with your child. First think of some characteristics you both agree are important – for example, honesty. On a piece of paper, draw a circle, then write what the characteristic feels like inside the circle. Then, outside the circle write what this characteristic looks like as behaviour or actions.

Sticking up for others

Honesty

Difficult

Brave

Telling the truth

ENCOURAGING OPEN-MINDEDNESS

Being open-minded about others helps a child to be themselves, because they understand the endless possibilities for their own lives. By encouraging them to take an interest in all the diverse kinds of people, families and relationships they see around themselves, you'll help them feel comfortable being their true, authentic self.

One way to help is to look at the role models your child has. It's worth looking to diverse books, games, TV and film to broaden your child's horizons.

When a child understands and respects the many differences and similarities we have with one another, they are able to form friendships with kids from all walks of life.

What you can and can't control

Worrying can get in the way of forming new friendships. Your child might worry about their own personality or appearance, as well as how potential friends might react to them.

One thing that can help calm anxiety is reminding your child what they can and cannot control.

Brainstorm with your child the things that they can control, and those they have little to no control over.

Some ideas to get you started: other people's thoughts, our own bravery, other people's actions, our own actions, other people's words... add your own.

When we understand that something is outside of our control, it can be easier to let it go and focus our energy on what we can control – our own thoughts and actions.

A growth mindset

A "growth mindset" is based on the idea that we can learn from mistakes and that skills can be improved with practice and perseverance.

A quick way of instilling a growth mindset in your child is to use the word "yet". When faced with a challenge or a negative thought, adding the word "yet" can often change a challenge into an opportunity and negativity into hopefulness.

For example, "I haven't made any friends" becomes "I haven't made any friends yet". While the difference is subtle, the word "yet" shows that change is possible and that your child has the power to change the things in their life they're unhappy about.

"Do they like me?"

When we meet a potential new friend, it's easy to become preoccupied over whether they like us. If your child is making new friends and worrying about being liked, try challenging them with the following question: do *you* like *them*? The answer is likely to be, "I'm not sure yet!"

Friendships are formed with mutual effort, rather than by a snap decision about the other's likeability based on first impressions. Compatibility is important too, but that emerges through spending time together. So, if your child truly wants to form a friendship with someone, it's up to them to take steps toward building it. Encourage them to initiate conversations, give compliments or invite them for a play date (see chapters 2 and 3 on social skills) to grow a friendship.

"No one likes me!"

It's a common complaint among children, but if your child repeatedly claims that "nobody likes me!" it's time to challenge this all-or-nothing thinking and shrink the problem back to its true size. Look for examples of people who genuinely like them (and remember, being liked and having friendships are two different things).

It's possible that your child is well-liked and has plenty of potential friends at their fingertips. Building friendships takes time and effort, and some social skills need to be learned. Being liked is the easy part!

The preferences game

Getting to know the kind of person they are will help grow your child's confidence and self-esteem. Try playing this simple game together. Which of each pair do you prefer? Which does your child pick? See what you share, where you differ and what conversations it sparks.

- **Cats or dogs?**
- **Quiet field or busy beach?**
- **Birthday presents or birthday party?**
- **Spring or autumn?**
- **Sweet or savoury?**
- **Climbing trees or building dens?**
- **Swimming or running?**
- **Saturday or Sunday?**
- **Breakfast or lunch?**
- **Reading or drawing?**

WRITE A LETTER

Write a letter to your child including some of the things you admire about them. Try starting with a short note recounting the day's events.

You dealt really well with...

You showed such kindness when...

You were brave when...

Make a habit of writing to your child every time you notice something admirable about them. It can be difficult for children to recognize their best qualities, so having someone who loves them point them out will help them to appreciate and learn about their personality.

When I feel most like myself

Where and when do you feel most like yourself? Think about this question for yourself and use it to start a conversation with your child about where they feel most like themselves. It could be a place, an activity or being with a certain person or group of people. Talk about how you both feel at those times, what you look forward to about them and what you can do to feel that way more often.

Identifying times when your child feels good about themselves, and what that feels like for them, is a great opportunity to learn more about them and boost their self-esteem.

Find an inspirational quote

Set aside some time with your child to look through books, magazines and on the internet for inspirational quotes. Once you find one (or a few!) that you both agree fits your child and helps them feel good about themselves, display the quote somewhere in your house, somewhere where they'll see it regularly. You might like to paint the words on a canvas, write them on a Post-it note or even try your hand at calligraphy to create something really beautiful and eye-catching.

Gratitude

Take turns with your child to say something you're grateful for. It can be anything! Big or small, from your healthy body to your cosy jumper. See if you can both keep coming up with ideas for the whole of the journey to school, or get into the habit of exchanging three things you're grateful for each evening before saying goodnight to each other.

Looking for the positives in life helps build self-esteem and mental well-being. Just like a muscle, if you practise gratitude regularly, your capacity for gratitude will grow.

LET YOUR CHILD TEACH YOU SOMETHING

A sense of mastery is a powerful way of building self-esteem. What is your child good at that you don't have the first clue about? It could be a computer game, a particular animal they're interested in or perhaps their favourite author. Give them the opportunity to teach you all about it.

Sit down together for 20–30 minutes and let your child take the lead. Ask plenty of questions and be really patient and curious.

CHAPTER 2

Social Skills

It's easy to assume that social skills come naturally. And to some, they do. For others, it's more difficult – social norms and expectations can be a bit baffling to children, but just like any other skill they can be learned. In this chapter we'll cover a number of skills that will come in useful for making friends and navigating relationships.

Give and take

Putting in the right amount of effort is an important skill in building friendships. Your child might feel anxious about being "too keen", but with a bit of gentle give and take, friendships can be made without one or the other child having to get too far out of their comfort zone.

Try it together: next time your child asks for something, get them to help out too. For example, if they ask you for a drink of water, you could get them to bring you their cup first. Show your child how good it feels to work together in small ways.

Trust

Trust is earned, and proving ourselves to be trustworthy involves acting with integrity and keeping promises. Good friendships come from trusting others and being trustworthy ourselves.

Try it together: challenge your child to make and keep a promise to themselves. It might be to draw a picture every day for a week, or do all of their homework before the weekend. Help them choose something that's realistic and they can motivate themselves to achieve. Keep track of how they're doing and celebrate their wins. If they drop the ball, remind them that it's OK to make mistakes, and to pick yourself up and try again.

JOINING IN

Including others in their games, conversations and interests is a quick way to gain friends. Encourage your child to share, invite others into their game and listen to other kids' ideas.

Try it together: invite your child to join in with some of your daily activities. Perhaps they could sit with you while you answer emails, help with the washing-up or join you on an errand. Equally, ask to join in with some of the things they do at home.

Conversation skills

There's no great secret to becoming a good conversationalist: it comes down to making the other person feel good speaking to you. Asking questions, listening carefully and taking an interest, while being yourself and offering your own viewpoint, all add up to a person who's a pleasure to talk to.

Try it together: invest in a set of conversation cards. Check out Fink Cards, The School of Life and Sussed for interesting decks to get you talking. Or, you could make your own using the topics covered in this book as conversation starters!

Interpreting body language

By the time we reach adulthood, most of us have learned to read body language quite naturally. However, children are still learning and may not be able to pick up on cues quite as easily. Around 93 per cent of communication is non-verbal, so helping your child read body language will boost their friendship-forming skills.

Try it together: narrate your body language. It might feel strange at first, but adding context to the way you're holding your body will help your child learn the outer signs of inner emotions. For example, if your shoulders are hunched, you could say, "Look at my shoulders, I'm so tense from work. I'll relax them now, that's better. I feel a bit calmer already."

Listening skills

When we listen well, the other person feels appreciated and respected. Some children might have trouble listening — perhaps they don't yet fully appreciate its value, or anxiety causes their minds to rush ahead to their response — and you can gently help them listen better.

Try it together: model good listening skills by using active listening when your child is talking to you. Turn toward them and come down to their level, give them your full attention and, when it is your turn to talk, repeat in your own words what they have told you, so they know you have heard and understood them.

Personal space

The amount of personal space we need varies from person to person, and can change with our mood. If your child has not yet learned the subtle art of giving appropriate personal space and "alone time", they might feel rejected or confused when others ask for it.

Try it together: talk about personal-space bubbles with your child. Stand at opposite ends of the room and imagine bubbles around yourselves. See how it feels to "shrink your bubbles" by taking steps slowly toward each other. Where feels comfortable? If and when you need more space, you could talk about how big your bubble is at that moment.

Kindness

Spreading kindness and having a sense of
social responsibility helps you feel connected
to the place you live and the people in your
community. When you feel connected to
others, friendships naturally follow.

Try it together: encourage kindness and community
by going litter-picking together at a nearby beach,
organizing a local book exchange or volunteering
for a community project.

SHARING

To many children, sharing doesn't come easily. If your child isn't a fan of sharing, it can be difficult to explain the upside. It can be useful to think of what your child might gain by sharing in any given situation. For example, sharing a toy with another child means they gain a new person in their game, who can add to the fun and will likely share their games or toys, too.

Try it together: when you or your child help each other with something, like a piece of homework, try talking about it in terms of sharing the work. When you do something together, you're sharing that moment. If your child shifts their understanding of sharing into a more positive, collaborative one, it becomes easier.

Taking turns

Having something all to yourself sounds excellent to a child, and those who struggle in social interactions can find it hard to understand why they'd want to take turns. Take a playful approach to help them learn the joy of sharing with others.

Try it together: take turns whispering into each other's ears. You could tell jokes, whisper kind comments, describe the most disgusting sandwich you can think of… anything really, just as long as you take turns!

Private vs public behaviour

How we behave in public differs from how we behave in our own homes. Your child might find it difficult to know what's appropriate in different situations, and it can be quite frustrating for children when they feel the rules have been changed without their knowledge.

Try it together: chat about expectations before you go out – especially if it's to somewhere new. Keep the conversation light and try not to single out your child. For example, "We're going to a new park today – it's the sort of place where running about is fine, but picking the flowers isn't allowed."

Respecting house rules

Every family has different rules or ways of doing things at home. Let your child know that they can ask you – or ask their friend's parent to call you – if there's anything they're not sure about or feel uncomfortable with while they're away from home. For example, screen-time rules might be different, or pets could be allowed in different parts of the house.

Try it together: it's a good idea to prepare your child for this if they're visiting a friend or relative's house. Explain to your child that it's OK if the rules are different – it doesn't mean that one family is right and the other is wrong.

How to be a good guest

The norms of being a guest in someone else's house can be hard for children to grasp! Help them to understand by giving them some basic rules to follow. It's a good idea to tailor these to your child – you know them best and the things they find easy and hard.

Try it together: come up with some rules that can apply anywhere and write them down. Here are some ideas to get you started:

- **Remember to say "hello", "goodbye", "please" and "thank you".**
- **Treat your friend's home, belongings and family members with respect.**
- **You need to follow your friend's family house rules.**

It's OK to ask your friend or their parent/carer if there's something you're not sure about or need help with.

How to join in

Asking to join in with another child's game is often the first step in making a new friend, and it takes a ton of bravery. Encourage your child to find the courage to join in with others by building their self-esteem. Remind them how fun and interesting they are, and that anyone would be lucky to have them as a friend.

Try it together: if your child finds this especially hard, you can switch it up. Bring a ball or Frisbee to the park and play with your child. If another child is showing interest in your game, invite them to join in! You could also try building a den in the woods, drawing with chalk on the pavement or even learning a dance together in public. As long as you pick somewhere there are other children and have lots of fun, you and your child will be magnetic!

HOW TO INITIATE FRIENDSHIP

Learning to initiate a game or conversation is a great skill. The trick is not to overthink it. We all like being asked questions about our interests and children are no different.

Try it together: encourage your child to be curious and ask open-ended questions like these:

- **"What's that?"**
- **"How did you make it?"**
- **"Which is your favourite?"**

If they see a child reading an interesting magazine or building something fascinating, asking a simple question is the easiest way to start building a rapport and potentially a friendship.

Consent and boundaries

You can teach your child about boundaries by being someone who respects both their own and others' boundaries. The way your child sees you act will inform how they treat themselves and others as they grow into an adult. Teaching a healthy attitude to boundaries naturally feeds into a healthy understanding of consent, which will serve your child well in all their relationships.

Try it together: when you set a boundary with your child – for example, when you say "no" to them – it's important that you hold that boundary. Do not back down in response to your child's sadness or anger. Empathize and explain your reasoning to help your child deal with the difficult feelings that may arise. It's a tough thing to do, but so worth it in the long run.

Fairness

Often life isn't fair, and it can really hurt children's feelings when they feel they haven't received fair treatment. While you're not able to protect them completely from it, acknowledging their feelings when you spot something they might find unfair will help them learn to cope with jealousy or resentment.

Try it together: you can say something like, "It doesn't feel fair that they got more ice cream. It's so hard when someone else gets more than you. Wouldn't it be great to have ice cream for every meal, or live in a house made of ice cream... what flavour would your room be?"

Being a good winner and a good loser

If winning or losing is hard for your child, the game they're playing can become more important than the friendships they're forming! Help them to cope with feelings of anger or embarrassment when they lose – and avoid gloating when they win – by playing games together and modelling good sportsmanship. If you sense your child getting frustrated, you can both take a break.

Try it together: choose short games with simple rules. The opportunity to play several rounds will mean you can practise both winning and losing together. Games like *Uno*, *Go Fish* or *Guess Who?* are a great place to start.

EMPATHY

Seeing things from another's perspective can be difficult for children. They are naturally the centre of their own universe, so it's very normal for them to need help with empathizing. Empathy is a friendship superpower because it enables you to understand others and not take their actions personally. The below exercise is useful if your child is feeling jealousy, anger, resentment or confusion toward someone else.

Try it together: ask your child to think of a way in which the other person is lucky. How about a way in which they're unlucky? Talk about what differences the lucky and unlucky circumstances might have made to the other person's life.

Tone of voice

Children are excellent at showing their emotions, and their tone of voice can often give a good indication of how they are feeling inside. Some children get quite loud when they're excited or happy, which can be confusing for others!

Try it together: if your child's tone of voice doesn't quite match up with their words, playfully point it out to them. You could say, "Oh! Your words said one thing but your voice was loud/growly/high-pitched, which made me feel... I wonder if that's what you meant?"

Saying "no"

There are lots of different kinds of "no". Sometimes our "no" needs to set a firm boundary, other times we want to say "no" with kindness to save hurting someone's feelings. Being able to say "no" is a vital part of any friendship, as it allows us to be ourselves.

Try it together: model saying "no" in different ways by drawing your child's attention to how and why you're saying it, as well as your tone of voice. For example:

- **A firm "no" with one hand raised in front of your chest.**

- **A friendly "That sounds fun, but I can't right now. Perhaps we could do… instead?"**

- **A be-true-to-yourself "No, thank you."**

CHAPTER 3

Activities to Develop Social Skills

Children make connections through play, and non-verbal social skills develop far earlier than verbal ones. The activities on the following pages have been carefully selected for their potential to teach social skills through play. The activities will spark conversation, help you learn about each other, encourage collaborative play, grow your child's confidence and teach co-operation.

WOULD YOU RATHER...

This game can be played anywhere, any time! It's a great conversation starter and will help build your child's creativity as well as their conversation skills. Make up would-you-rather scenarios that are funny, gross or thought-provoking, and use them as icebreakers with potential new friends.

Here are a few to get you started:

- **Would you rather live with a toad or have a slug for a boss?**
- **Would you rather have a toe for a nose or noses for fingers?**
- **Would you rather go on holiday to a swamp or go to school in a haunted house?**

Play 20 questions

This classic game will develop your child's conversation skills, as well as helping them learn to read body language and play by the rules.

How to play: Person One thinks of a person, place or thing, and does not tell Person Two. Person Two must ask "yes" or "no" questions to work out what Person One is thinking of. If Person Two guesses correctly after the 20 questions, they get to answer the 20 questions in the next round.

Mirror drawing

This simple game teaches reciprocity and co-operation. It's also a great game to play with kids who struggle with talking.

You will need: one piece of paper and two pens.

How to play: draw a line down the middle of the paper. Person One draws on one side, while Person Two draws on the other side of the line as if in a mirror. Keep going until Person Two decides the drawing is complete, then turn over the paper and swap roles.

Compliments game

Learning how to give and receive compliments can be tricky for some children. This game will take the pressure off and help them get creative and positive about how they view themselves and others.

How to play: you can play in a group or just the two of you. If you're in a group, take turns saying something nice about one of the other people you're with, but don't reveal who it's for. The others must guess who the compliment is for. If you're playing one-on-one, agree on a list of people to compliment and guess, such as cousins or neighbours.

Start a club

A shared interest is one of the best icebreakers at any age. Whether your child is into coding, drawing or skateboarding, someone you know is bound to have a child who's also mad about it, or eager to learn.

How to do it: use your own social networks to find like-minded children with similar interests to your child, and organize a meet-up so they can share knowledge, get to know each other and play together. If the first meet-up's a success, make a regular thing of it.

Power poses

Power poses work by moving your body as if you are feeling very confident, which sends signals to the brain, increasing feelings of confidence. It's a good idea for your child to learn one or two of their favourite power poses, as they're a great confidence booster to prepare for daunting social situations.

How to do it: practise power poses together – side by side in front of a full-length mirror, or face to face, mirroring each other! Poses you might like to try include:

- **Hands on hips like Wonder Woman.**
- **One hand raised like the Statue of Liberty.**
- **Stretching out your limbs to make a star shape.**

FIND YOUR SUPERPOWERS

If your child uses unkind words about themselves, pay close attention to these words. Talk kindly and playfully about them, and see how you could shift your child's view of themselves to something more positive. This activity will help your child to challenge negative self-talk and build their self-esteem.

How to play: take the negative word and write it in the centre of a piece of paper. Together, make a mind map of all the different things you associate with it. Can you find a superpower? For example, "I'm too sensitive" becomes "I have super-sensing powers". You could have fun creating a costume, origin story and nemesis for your child's superhero alter ego.

Fortunately, unfortunately

This is a great, funny game for creating both stories and friendships. It requires both players to think outside the box and riff off each other's creativity. Try it with your child to build their confidence and ability to take turns.

How to play: this game can be played by two or more players. One person starts with a simple sentence like, "One day I went to the beach." After this, take turns adding a sentence to the story. The catch is, every sentence must begin with the word "fortunately" or "unfortunately" alternately, making a story that twists and turns with every sentence!

Step-by-step stories

A step-by-step story is a visual guide to a real-life situation that your child may struggle with, like a new club they are joining or a school trip they are worried about. Often used by people on the autistic spectrum, they can help show your child what to expect and how to navigate the tricky world of friendships.

Try it at home: break the situation down into stages and illustrate each stage using simple pictures and words, like a comic strip. Make sure your step-by-step story shows your child what order things will happen in, who will be with them and what to expect.

Conversation starters

A simple question can spark off a great conversation. Here are a few your child can arm themselves with. With these plus a bit of bravery, your child can talk to anyone!

- **What's the worst thing about being ___ years old?**

- **What's the best thing about being ___ years old?**

- **If you could change one thing about the world, what would it be?**

- **What magic power do you wish you had?**

- **What's one thing you're really good at?**

- **What's something you'd like to learn how to do?**

Eye contact and body language

Making eye contact can be a real struggle for some children, and it's something that can have a big effect on how we relate to one another. Learning to make appropriate eye contact will also ensure your child picks up on all sorts of body language and non-verbal communication.

How to play: stand with your child in front of the mirror and make silly faces at each other. Keep eye contact and act out emotions for each other to guess.

Role-play social situations

Role-playing tricky social situations can be a big help when it comes to anxious kids. They'll have a chance to express their worries and plan how they'd react in a variety of circumstances.

How to do it: you can role-play anything – from parts of your daily routine to one-off scenarios to approaching potential new friends. Act out the situation and follow your child's lead. You can run through several different outcomes – best-case scenarios as well as worst-case ones. Try switching roles to give your child the chance to see another perspective.

TIP
50

Scavenger hunt

To develop your child's listening and observation skills, try sending them on a scavenger hunt around the house. It's a great game to play on a play date too. Give specific instructions and make it fun. For an extra twist, you could ask them to find sounds too! Here's a list of ideas to get you started:

- **Something made of wood**
- **Something older than you are**
- **Something that starts with the letter "E"**
- **Something smaller than a paper clip**
- **Something with six sides**
- **Something that makes a noise**
- **Something red you can wear**

CHAPTER 4

Emotions

Emotions make us who we are. While it's important for your child to feel comfortable being themselves, being around someone who's expressing big emotions can be uncomfortable. The ability to regulate their emotions is something children develop over time and at different paces. If your child struggles with certain emotions or situations, read on for advice on how to help build their emotional regulation skills.

Stretch

Stretching is a quick way to help your body and mind regulate emotions. Stretching releases tension and makes your body feel better instantly, which has a knock-on effect on the mind and the central nervous system that controls our emotions.

Next time you see your child struggling with a big emotion, encourage them to stretch with you. If you can get outside to do it, all the better. There's no need to learn any complex techniques (unless your child is interested in yoga), simply letting your body guide you as to what feels good – and supporting your child to do the same – will help them regain a sense of equilibrium.

Breathe

Much like stretching, breathing deeply calms the body, which helps regulate the central nervous system. When we pay attention to our breath, we are able to access greater confidence, mental clarity and emotional balance.

When your child is calm, teach them a breathing technique such as "hand breathing". As you trace your right index finger slowly up your left thumb, breathe in. Breathe out as your finger traces down the other side of your thumb. Repeat for each finger.

RHYTHMIC MOVEMENT

When children are able to regulate their emotions, they are able to relate to others, share, have reciprocal conversations and make friends. If and when your child becomes overwhelmed with strong emotions (you might call this a tantrum or a meltdown), they do not have access to the parts of the brain needed for relating to others.

Research has shown that rhythmic movement can help your child back into an emotionally regulated state. Try bouncing on a trampoline, running or drumming as a way to calm down. Do these things together and don't worry about looking silly – humour also helps to break the tension.

What's holding your child back?

Ask your child: "What do you find difficult about friendships?"

They might answer in a myriad of different ways. Pay attention to what they say and the words they use. If they talk about the behaviour of others, perhaps they've been burned by past experiences. If they mention perceived flaws in their own personality or appearance, it's probably a good idea to build their self-esteem more.

The more you can understand your child, their experiences and the way they view themselves and others, the more able you'll be to help and support them.

Fear of rejection

Fear of rejection can be one of the biggest barriers to making friends. Building your child's self-esteem will help with the sting of this — you can't 100 per cent protect your child from rejection, sadly. Sometimes another child is simply not a good fit for friendship with your child and that's OK.

Let your child know that they might get rejected in life and in friendships. When we open our hearts to others, it makes us vulnerable. But closing our hearts means we never get to make those connections. If your child gets their feelings hurt, let them feel hurt — don't dismiss their pain. Empathize with and validate their feelings, and tell them that they will cope, that you love them unconditionally and that who they are is OK.

HANDLING REJECTION

Rejection is a part of life – no matter how much we'd like to protect our children from it, we can't. It's hard to deal with at any age, and helping your child to learn healthy ways to cope with rejection is a gift they will come back to again and again throughout their life.

If your child has been rejected by a friend – or even if they're just *feeling* rejected – it helps to acknowledge the pain inherent in this. Try to avoid brushing over their feelings or encouraging them to look on the bright side. Let them know that it's OK to talk about these difficult feelings and also that we must respect others when they tell us "no".

Handling embarrassment

Some children can get embarrassed easily, which can lead to shyness or social withdrawal. When your child feels embarrassed, cringe with them. Name and validate their uncomfortable emotions, and empathize by talking about a time you felt embarrassed.

If your child gets embarrassed in social situations or when trying something new, it might feel like an uphill battle helping them make friends. It's OK to acknowledge the embarrassing moment next time the situation comes up and to help your child take steps to avoid that embarrassment happening again. Let them know that everyone feels that way sometimes and that it's not a sign they've done something wrong.

Handling anger

Anger is often a difficult emotion to express
and to be around. It's a perfectly healthy and
normal feeling, and guiding your child toward
expressing it in healthy and respectful
ways will serve them well for life.

Help them identify anger by naming and validating
it yourself: "I think you're feeling angry, it's really
upsetting when others don't want to share."

Pay attention to how they're expressing anger,
and redirect any problematic behaviour: "Feeling
angry is OK, but hitting me isn't. If your
body needs to hit, hit this sofa."

Handling jealousy

Jealousy strikes when someone else has something we think we deserve. When we're feeling jealous, it can manifest as negative thoughts toward the person we are jealous of, rather than positive thoughts about the thing we desire.

When your child expresses jealousy in this way, try to reframe their perspective into something more positive. You could say, "She looks so cool! It would be great if you had trainers like that. What colour would you choose?" Once you've taken the focus off the other person, a conversation about the thing your child wants can happen.

Handling unrequited feelings

It can be really hard for children to understand when someone doesn't feel the same as them. Perhaps they don't want to be friends, or they simply don't want to play the same thing as your child that day.

Start by listening to and validating their feelings. They might be feeling sadness, anger, disappointment… all very normal. Then, reassure them that other people's choices aren't about your child. Just because their friend didn't want to play football today, it doesn't mean either of them have done something wrong. Help them understand by talking about a time you or they made a similar choice.

HANDLING ANXIETY

Many children struggle with anxiety and it can be a barrier to forming new friendships. If you sense that your child is feeling anxious, you could say, "I feel like you're anxious right now, is that right?" Doing so will help your child learn to recognize when anxiety is clouding their thoughts and affecting their emotions.

The things that make us feel anxious vary greatly from person to person. Learn what's hard for your child, acknowledge how difficult they find it and use techniques such as the exercises on pages 66, 67 and 68 to help them deal with anxiety and find their inner confidence.

Handling change

Change presents unique challenges. Even small changes can knock a sensitive child off-kilter, and big life changes – like moving house or changing schools – can affect their friendships, too.

When there's a change coming up, give your child as much notice as possible. Talk about it and listen to their worries, hopes and objections. If possible, give your child a chance to do a "dry run" using role-play or by visiting the new place. Acknowledge that you can't guarantee everything will turn out how they want it to, and focus on the fact that they can and will cope with whatever comes.

Handling disappointment

When a child experiences disappointment it can discourage them from trying again. Acknowledge and feel their disappointment with them. Let them know it's OK to feel let down. Try not to encourage self-blame or unfair blaming of others.

Once the initial feelings have lightened, look for what can be learned from the disappointment. Help them recognize the fact that they deserve good friends, and that someone else's actions — or even a mistake, failure or rejection — in no way diminishes their worth as a person.

CHAPTER 5

Being, Choosing and Keeping Good Friends

Friendships are about more than people just spending time in each other's company. They require compatibility and vulnerability to initiate, as well as effort and care to maintain. Learning how to recognize the characteristics of a good friend in another person is as important as cultivating them in ourselves. And once your child finds a good friendship, help them put in the work to keep it.

Quality over quantity

Being 'popular' can feel like a big deal for children and young people. If your child has one or two good, solid friendships already, it's worth thinking critically and discussing whether they truly need more. It's always a good idea to develop social skills and meet new people, but a preoccupation with popularity can have a negative effect on self-esteem.

You can use the tools in this chapter to help your child better understand the friendships they already have, as well as to make smart choices when it comes to making new friends.

What makes a good friend?

Take some time to chat about each of the characteristics that make a good friend. Do you agree with this list? Would you add anything or take anything away?

You might ask questions like: "Who comes to mind for each one?", "Can you have a good friendship if one or both of you don't have this characteristic?" and "Do you have this characteristic?"

- **Trustworthy**
- **Honest**
- **A good listener**
- **A sense of humour**
- **Something in common**
- **Supportive**
- **Empathetic**

WHAT KIND OF PERSON DO YOU WANT AS A FRIEND?

On the previous page, we looked at the essential characteristics of a good friend. Now, let's think about what kind of person your child would like to be friends with. You could ask them in conversation or see if they'd like to write a sentence or two for each question.

- **What interests would you like a friend to have?**
- **How would you like to play or spend time with a friend?**
- **What is the most important thing you look for in a friend?**

What do friends do?

Being friends is more than just liking each other – friendship is something you *do*. Take some time to think out loud with your child about the kinds of things friends do with or for one another.

It can be helpful to think about how you treat a friend differently to someone you only know a little bit.

Come up with some ideas together. Here are a few examples to get you started:

A friend...

- **... says hello when they see you.**
- **... plays with you.**
- **... sticks up for you against bullies.**

Friendships online

The internet can add new and unfamiliar sides to children's friendships. Whether it's a friend from real life that they're chatting with online, or someone they're playing with on the internet, it's important to maintain those boundaries around personal information, and pay attention to websites' age restrictions and privacy settings. Let your child know that if someone tries to pressure them into relaxing internet-safety rules, it's a cause for concern and they should tell you straight away.

Make sure your child knows about internet safety – you could work together to draw up an agreement or set of rules. There are some great resources online at www.childnet.com.

Social media and self-esteem

If your child uses social media, or you're thinking about letting them, it's worth researching and being aware of the effect it can have on self-esteem. If great importance is placed on the number of social media friends, followers or likes your child can accumulate, they can start to rely on these things as a source of self-worth and their confidence can plummet as a result.

Coupled with the preoccupation with appearance that is common on social networks, it can be an unhealthy place for your child to conduct their social life.

Don't be afraid to take your time, set rules around privacy settings, be one of your child's followers and to say "no" if something doesn't feel right.

PLAY DATES

When your child invites a friend round, make sure you follow a few simple rules to help it run smoothly.

- **Have an activity up your sleeve that they'll both enjoy – just in case they get bored.**

- **Tell the friend where the toilet is – a lot of children are scared to ask!**

- **Relax about table manners – don't accept disrespect, but be aware that these vary so much, and it can create a lot of tension if you're considerably stricter than what the friend is used to.**

Other than that, it's best to let them get on with it.

Making friends outside of school

If your child is looking beyond their schoolmates for friendships, get creative in your approach to helping them. Look to your wider social circle – do you have an acquaintance whose offspring share similar interests to yours? Get them together for a casual play date!

Look online for local clubs – there's a lot out there, and it's not just sport that's on offer. Coding, archaeology and art clubs can be great places to find like-minded children.

Your local neighbourhood can also be a source of new friends. Keep your eyes peeled for potential friends and make an effort to start a conversation with them or their parents if you see them out and about.

Teachers' role in friendships

The social dynamics of a class have a big effect on the atmosphere of a classroom and how well the children can learn. So, teachers are naturally aware of the friendships within their classes, and supporting children with making and maintaining healthy friendships is within their remit.

Don't hesitate to talk to your child's teacher if you're concerned about any aspect of your child's friendships at school. Communication is key and teachers can offer valuable insight, advice and strategies. When you work together with your child's teacher, your child feels supported both at home and at school.

Being friendly vs being friends

It's important your child understands that they have a choice in whom they spend time with — feeling secure in this knowledge will help them choose healthy friendships and relationships later on in life. They don't have to be friends with everyone and they don't have to accept all offers of friendship either.

However, it's important to treat others with respect and an element of friendliness. Striking this balance can be hard, so keep an open dialogue with your child, and they'll feel comfortable talking to you about any and all aspects of friendship.

CHAPTER 6

Dealing with Fallouts, Bad Friends and Bullying

All friendships experience conflict and it's not a sign of a bad or weak friendship – quite the opposite! However, there are such things as bad friends and even bullies that call themselves friends. Help your child learn to tell the difference by giving them the skills to tolerate and resolve conflict, while making choices based on their own well-being.

Allowing others to feel their feelings

When there's conflict – big or small – in a friendship, many of us want to resolve it as quickly as possible. It can be confusing and upsetting for children when they say sorry and their apology isn't accepted.

Sometimes the best thing is to leave the other person to their feelings. Help your child work out the right thing for them to do – whether that's apologizing or telling their friend that they feel hurt or upset by their actions. However, you can't control how the other person will react, so giving them space to feel their feelings is often a good idea. Hopefully, when they're ready, the conflict can be resolved.

Conflict resolution

Once your child and their friend are both ready to talk about what happened, encourage your child to be brave and start the conversation. Here are some great rules to help your child have difficult conversations after a fallout:

- **Use "I" statements – your child should focus on how they personally felt about what happened.**
- **Take turns speaking and listening, without interrupting.**
- **Try to understand each other's point of view.**
- **Agree on how you could both do things differently in future.**

If your child learns to resolve conflicts in this way, the friendships they make will be all the stronger, healthier and more rewarding for it.

If your child is bullied

Being bullied is a terrible thing for a child to deal with. It can come in the form of physical, verbal or emotional bullying. One of the worst things about bullying is that the victim can sometimes feel like they deserve the treatment they are receiving and not recognize it for what it is. They might feel embarrassed or assume it's their fault.

If you suspect or know your child is being bullied, let them know that it isn't their fault and they don't deserve to be treated in this way. Speak to the parent/carer/teacher and stand up for your child until the problem is dealt with.

If you see another child being bullied

What counts as bullying? Chat with your child and see what they think is and isn't bullying behaviour.

If your child saw someone being bullied, what would they do?

It can be a frightening situation to be in, so talking about a plan of action is often helpful. Here's a guide to get you and your child started:

- **If you feel safe, tell the bully to stop it.**
- **Ask the victim if they are OK.**
- **Help the victim find a safe adult or friend, or fetch one yourself.**
- **Tell an adult what happened.**
- **If you're friends with the bully, consider whether you still want them as a friend.**

IF YOUR CHILD IS BULLYING OTHERS

If you find out your child has been bullying others, it can be very painful. It's tempting to blame yourself as a parent, but try to be kind to yourself.

Inform your child's teacher (or the responsible adult where the bullying is taking place). A good teacher will be able to support both children appropriately.

Talk to your child in a non-judgemental, calm and compassionate way. Bullying behaviour can often be a sign of a child with low self-esteem or painful emotions. Listen to what they say and pay attention to the feelings that lie beneath their words. Support your child to make amends and to grow their self-esteem in healthy ways.

If your child's friend is bullying them

Here's a list of things that friends definitely don't – or shouldn't – do to each other. Chat with your child about the things on this list, and feel free to add your own.

- **Upset you on purpose**
- **Hurt you physically**
- **Laugh at you when you're upset**
- **Lie to you**
- **Call you unkind names**
- **Steal from you**
- **Touch you inappropriately**
- **Put pressure on you to do something you don't want to do**
- **Try to control what you do or think**

If your child experiences any of these things from another child, discuss with them why it's wrong and let them know they don't have to put up with it. If you have concerns, it's a good idea to get in touch with the child's school or another relevant adult.

What makes a bad friend?

There's a difference between bullying and simply being a bad friend. Talk to your child about these friendship no-nos so they can spot them in potential friends, or even in themselves.

A bad friend...

- **... only spends time with you to use your toys or video games.**

- **... doesn't feel good to be around.**

- **... tries to change things about your appearance or personality.**

- **... is only friends with you when no one else is around.**

Can you come up with any more?

WHAT TO DO IF YOUR CHILD HAS A BAD FRIEND

If your child has a friend who's treating them badly, annoying them, or simply doesn't feel like a good match... it's best for them to firstly talk it through with each other.

Encourage your child to tell their friend how they feel and what isn't working in their friendship. The way the other person reacts is often a good indicator of how much they value the friendship and how much they respect your child. When you think about it this way, your child doesn't have anything to lose (except a bad friend!) by being honest.

Once they've had a chance to talk it through, your child can decide whether they want to keep, tone down or end the friendship.

How we talk about others

When your child is upset with a friend, or a friendship has ended, they might feel tempted to speak unkindly or disrespectfully about their ex-friend.

Help them understand that even if a friend has hurt them, it's still not OK to share their personal information, tell lies or spread rumours about them.

Sure, they can vent their feelings to you or a trusted friend. Their feelings are valid. Alongside this, help them understand that treating all human beings with respect is how we show respect for ourselves.

Peer pressure

Children want to fit in and feel a sense of belonging and identity. However, this can turn into peer pressure – your child might believe their appearance, personality or interests need to be the same as their friends'.

It can help to arm your child with some strategies for when they feel pressured into something they're uncomfortable with:

- **Make a joke – laughing it off can break the tension and gently get someone to back off.**
- **Say they don't want to get into trouble.**
- **Ignore it.**
- **Walk away.**
- **Say "no" firmly.**
- **Ask friends to back them up.**

Let them know that they can always talk to you about things that make them feel uncomfortable.

When to tell an adult

Learning when to tell an adult about another child's behaviour can be really tricky. Getting the right balance between building resilience and asking for help is different for every child and at every age.

Ask your child what they would do in the following situations:

- **Someone is hurt.**
- **Someone's not taking turns.**
- **Someone made a rude face.**

Would they let it go, try to resolve it themselves or tell an adult? You could also talk about situations they've been in or witnessed before — would they do anything differently if it happened again?

THINGS THAT WILL LOSE FRIENDS

While you want your child to be themselves, there are some behaviours that aren't fun to be around and can lose friends. To help your child understand what type of behaviour might lead to this, start by discussing these ones:

What's the difference between...

- **... being confident and being bossy?**
- **... being proud of yourself and being a show-off?**
- **... being good at something and being over-competitive?**
- **... being knowledgeable and being a know-it-all?**

Come up with scenarios together that show the two sides of each example.

Apologizing and taking responsibility

"Sorry" is a small word, but it's a big deal when it comes to friendships. If your child has done something wrong or upset their friend, saying sorry takes real courage.

To apologize effectively, your child should acknowledge what they did and ask how they can make it up to their friend.

Here's a simple script to help repair a friendship:

I'm sorry for...

How can I make it up to you?

Next time I'll...

There's often hurt on both sides when a fallout happens, so let your child know that their feelings are valid, too, and that nobody is perfect.

Ending a friendship

Ending a friendship should always be your child's (or their friend's) decision. It may be helpful to let them know that they don't have to continue a friendship they are unhappy in, but support them to make their own choices and reassure them that you'll be there for them whatever they choose.

If they ask for your support to end a friendship, help them plan what to say or perhaps write a letter.

Empower your child to say "no" to bad friendships, by reminding them they are worthy of good ones!

CHAPTER 7

Looking to Yourself

Giving your child skills, tools, opportunities and resources to form new friendships is valuable and never wasted. It's also useful to think about the example you are setting, and your own attitudes, tastes and patterns in friendships. As adults, we often put a lot of thought into our romantic relationships. In this chapter we'll look at how you can use your own experiences and social skills to model healthy friendships.

Keeping open communication

Being the kind of parent that your child feels able to talk freely with can be a difficult balancing act, but it's so worth it.

Talk about your feelings, experiences and relationships as if they matter (because they do!) and your child will learn that theirs do, too. Listen with an open mind and love with an open heart. Treat your child with respect – this includes respecting them enough to let them take responsibility for their words, choices and actions.

Appreciate and honour your child in all their fullness and complexity and they'll feel comfortable coming to you with whatever is on their mind.

Giving your child feedback

As parents and carers, we can get in the habit of putting our feelings last. It's true that reacting with anger or upset to our children's actions is usually not the best thing to do. However, when we give ourselves a chance to speak calmly to our children about how we feel, we can help them learn valuable social skills.

The trick with this is to speak about your child's behaviour, rather than who they are as a person. "When you leave dirty socks on the floor, I feel frustrated and disrespected," is more constructive than, "You always leave dirty socks on the floor! You are so disrespectful."

HOW TO LISTEN TO AND EMPATHIZE WITH YOUR CHILD

Good listening skills are the key to being the type of parent your child will feel safe and comfortable confiding in.

Listen carefully when your child speaks to you – put down other tasks or turn off screens so you can give them your full attention.

Validate any feelings they have – tell them that their feelings are understandable and make sense.

Reflect back what you hear – rephrase slightly and help them name their emotions. This way they'll be sure you've understood.

Ask how you can help – does your child want to look for solutions, or just to talk it through? Let them guide you.

Think back to your own childhood friendships

To our adult ears, the conflicts and complexities of children's friendships can sound petty. When you catch yourself judging in this way, think back to yourself at that age. Can you remember how important, real and significant your friendships and their resulting drama felt? Use these memories to empathize with and validate your child's feelings, offering advice and an adult perspective later.

Show your child that what's important to them is important to you, and they will grow up confident that their feelings and relationships matter.

Screen time

A lot of attention is given to children's screen time, but what about adults'?

When we let phones and tablets take our attention away mid-conversation, mid-meal or even mid-sentence, we are teaching our children not only that it's OK way to behave this way with others, but also that our screens come before them.

As so many essential tasks can now be performed on our smartphones, it's important to acknowledge that we aren't just mindlessly scrolling *every* time we look at our phones. We might be paying a bill, emailing school or making an appointment. (Also, there's nothing wrong with mindless scrolling, in moderation!)

Try to form good habits around screen-based distractions and complete screen-based tasks at a set time each day.

Model good social skills

You can model good social skills any time. Conversations around the dinner table, speaking to strangers and dealing with conflict are things that come up in our lives every day; we just need to keep our eyes open for opportunities.

Look for such opportunities when you're with your child. Perhaps you need to ask for directions, complain about a meal in a restaurant or relieve boredom on a family car trip. All of these interactions between you and other people are chances to practise and model social skills. Seeing the advice in this book play out in real life will give your child a deeper understanding of how to build relationships, stand up for themselves and treat others with respect.

OBSERVE OTHER FRIENDSHIPS

The world around us can be a brilliant tool for learning about social interaction and relationships. When you're out and about with your child, try wondering out loud (but not *too* loud!) about the people around you.

"They look excited to see each other!"

"That boy looks upset — what do you think happened?"

"Those two girls look like best friends — what do you think they like doing together?"

This simple exercise will help expand your child's knowledge of friendships and relationships, as well as helping them imagine the types of friendships they'd like to have.

Pay attention to your friendships

Show your child how to make and cultivate good friendships by paying attention to the friendships in your life, too. Kids don't always think to ask about their parents' lives outside of the family, so take the initiative to talk about your social life and how you maintain friendships, deal with disagreements, keep in touch and the kinds of things you expect in a friendship.

Share photos of you and your friends and talk about how friendships change over a lifetime. Teach them about the effort involved, as well as the value gained from strong friendships.

Different friendship appetites

It can be tempting to hope your child will make lots and lots of friends, but it's important to recognize that everyone has different appetites for friendship. Some – often more extroverted people – like to have a high number of friendships, while the more introverted among us value a smaller group of close friends, or a best friend as well as a few more casual friendships.

If your child has a couple of good friendships in their life, they're already doing really well!

WHEN TO STEP IN, WHEN TO LEAVE IT

For the most part, it's best to follow your child's lead when it comes to existing friendships. There are, however, certain instances where stepping in is the responsible thing to do.

Everyone's boundaries will be different, so trust yourself to set these. A few situations to consider as non-negotiables are: bullying, drugs, coercion or illegal activity. Also, if a friendship seems to be negatively affecting your child's mental health, it's OK to voice your concerns.

Guiding your child toward healthy friendships, while allowing them to make their own choices, is sometimes a fine line to tread. Trust yourself to know the right thing to do.

When you disapprove of your child's friends

So, your child has made friends with the one child in their class you were hoping they wouldn't. Unfortunately, in this situation, this is the time to keep your opinions to yourself and let your child make their own decisions.

Any actions you might take to control the friendship will likely backfire and, in general, having friends that are unlike your family members is a healthy and appropriate step toward independence.

If the friendship turns sour, resist the urge to say "I told you so" and support your child in the same way you otherwise would.

Separation anxiety

We are our children's safety, and sometimes they want to hold on to us like a comfort blanket! If your child struggles with saying goodbye or being away from you, here are a few strategies that may help:

- **A "hug button" drawn on their hand.**
- **A small stone or piece of fabric to keep in their pocket.**
- **An object of yours (like a pen or a key ring) for them to look after until you return.**

Separation anxiety can be painful for both you and your child, so be kind to yourself and don't be afraid to ask for help making those transitional moments easier.

Book recommendations

There are some great books on friendships and social skills out there aimed at specific ages and topics. Here are a few you might find useful:

The Friendship Maze by Tanith Carey

Social Skills Activities for Kids by Natasha Daniels

How to be a Friend by Laurie Krasny Brown

Stand Up for Yourself & Your Friends
by Patti Kelley Criswell

*The Shyness and Social Anxiety Workbook
for Teens* by Jennifer Shannon

Staying Safe Online by Louie Stowell

The Floor is Lava by Ivan Brett

When to seek extra support

If your child's friendships or difficulty making friends is starting to have a negative effect on their mental health, it's a good idea to reach out for extra support.

Your child's teacher will be able to offer a different insight into their social life, as well as advice and a professional opinion.

Making an appointment with your doctor is another good step – they can offer advice and refer you to the best services and organizations to support your child's mental health and emotional well-being.

The YoungMinds' Parents Helpline can offer advice for parents, emotional support and signposting. Call 0808 802 5544 or find out more at www.youngminds.org.uk.

Conclusion

I hope you've found some useful ideas and encouragement in this book. There's certainly no one-size-fits-all blueprint for friendships, and your child will surprise you again and again with their ever-evolving personality and interests.

By taking an interest in your child's social development and guiding them toward a greater understanding of the way we build good relationships, you're giving them the best chance at growing into a strong, resilient adult capable of forming healthy, lasting friendships.

Always remember that your child is not alone and neither are you. There are so many wonderful friendships just waiting to be discovered. Every time you connect with your child in the spirit of humility and empathy, you build their self-esteem and ability to connect with others.

Notes

HELP YOUR CHILD MANAGE THEIR MOODS

Louise Baty

ISBN: 978-1-78783-674-7

£9.99 UK, $13.99 US, $15.99 CAN

LEARN TO TALK TO YOUR CHILD ABOUT THEIR BIG FEELINGS

We can all feel overwhelmed by big feelings, and this is especially true for children. They are still developing their emotional awareness and may struggle to manage their moods. While there's nothing wrong with an emotionally sensitive child, it can make life a little more difficult for them if they become easily frustrated, cry more readily and experience low self-esteem and feelings of powerlessness. This guide will teach you the skills to nurture your child's ability to notice, regulate and articulate their feelings in healthy, adaptive ways.

HELP YOUR CHILD DE-STRESS

Vicki Vrint

ISBN: 978-1-78783-673-0

£9.99 UK, $13.99 US, $15.99 CAN

72% OF CHILDREN SHOW BEHAVIOURS LINKED TO STRESS

Small amounts of stress are normal, but it can be difficult to know how best to support a child when they feel overwhelmed with worry. This practical guide offers strategies to help alleviate the physical symptoms and emotional signs of stress. By adopting simple tips, lifestyle changes and mood-boosting activities, you can help your child overcome challenging situations and live a happy and more carefree life.

Have you enjoyed this book?

If so, why not write a review on your favourite
website? If you're interested in finding out
more about our books, find us on Facebook at
Summersdale Publishers and follow us
on Twitter at @Summersdale.

Thanks very much for buying this
Summersdale book.

www.summersdale.com